This book is to be returned on or before
the last date stamped below.

What's Living in Your Garden?

Andrew Solway

Heinemann
LIBRARY

H www.heinemann.co.uk/library

Visit our website to find out more information about **Heinemann Library** books.

To order:

☎ Phone 44 (0) 1865 888066

▤ Send a fax to 44 (0) 1865 314091

▤ Visit the Heinemann Bookshop at www.heinemann.co.uk/library to browse our catalogue and order online.

First published in Great Britain by Heinemann Library, Halley Court, Jordan Hill, Oxford OX2 8EJ, part of Harcourt Education.
Heinemann is a registered trademark of Harcourt Education Ltd.

Editorial: Nancy Dickmann and Tanvi Rai
Design: David Poole and Paul Myerscough
Illustrations: Geoff Ward
Picture Research: Rebecca Sodergren
Production: Séverine Ribierre

Originated by Dot Gradations
Printed and bound in China by South China Printing Company

The paper used to print this book comes from sustainable resources.

ISBN 0 431 18965X
09 08 07 06 05 04
10 9 8 7 6 5 4 3 2 1

British Library Cataloguing in Publication Data

Solway, Andrew
Hidden Life: What's Living in Your Garden?
579.1'7554
A full catalogue record for this book is available from the British Library.

Acknowledgements
The publishers would like to thank the following for permission to reproduce photographs:

Alamy Images p. **17t**; Corbis p. **20t** (Sally A. Morgan, Ecoscene); Liz Eddison pp. **4**, **20b**; Holt Studio International pp. **8**, **14**; Science Photo Library p. **19t**; Science Photo Library p. **6**, **13**, **27** (Dr Jeremy Burgess), p. **7** (Martin Dohrn), p. **22t** (Georgette Douwma), p. **8t** (Ken Eward), p. **18** (Eye of Science), pp. **10b**, **12t**, **13t** (Vaughan Fleming), p. **22b** (Eric Grave), pp. **19b**, **21b**, **23** (Manfred Kage), p. **9** (James King-Holmes), p. **5t** (R. Maisonneuve, Publiphoto Diffusion), p. **5b** (Astrid and Hanns Freider Michler), p. **17b** (Microfield Scientific Ltd), p. **24** (Dr David Patterson), pp. **15**, **16** (David Scharf), pp. **10t**, **11** (Andrew Syred), pp. **25t**, **25b** (John Walsh).

Cover photograph of the head of a springtail, reproduced with permission of Science Photo Library/David Scharf.

Disclaimer

The paper used to print this book comes from sustainable resources.

Contents

Any words appearing in the text in bold, **like this**, are explained in the Glossary.

Many of the photos in this book were taken using a microscope. In the captions you may see a number that tells you how much they have been enlarged. For example, a photo marked '(x200)' is about 200 times bigger than in real life.

Taking a closer look

A garden has life everywhere. There are flowers, shrubs and trees growing in the soil; bees and other insects visiting the flowers; and birds and **mammals** eating the insects and plants. Sometimes there is a pond, with tadpoles and frogs. But if you look closer, you will find another whole world – hidden life that is only visible through a magnifying glass or a microscope.

Plant residents

Put a magnifying glass over your plants and you might spot tiny spider-like creatures called **mites**. They live by sucking sap from plants. Even smaller are the tiny **roundworms** that live on most plants. Some of them live on the plant surface, while others burrow into the leaves or roots.

The plants in the garden depend on microbes and other tiny creatures that enrich the soil.

With a microscope, you will be able to find **microbes** on the surface of plants. Many of them do the plant no harm, but some can cause plant diseases. The main culprits are **fungi**, relatives of mushrooms and toadstools.

Living dirt

Dig over the soil in the garden and you will probably turn up earthworms, centipedes, beetles and other minibeasts. But there are a whole range of microbes that live in the soil as well. Between them they do an important job, breaking down dead plant and animal material into useful **nutrients**. These nutrients become part of the soil and help plants to grow. And the microbes themselves are food for the soil minibeasts, which in turn get eaten by bigger animals such as birds, moles, hedgehogs and shrews.

Electron microscopes are expensive and complicated to use. But they have helped scientists to get a close look at even the tiniest bacteria.

A light microscope is easy to use, and it is possible to look at tiny, live creatures.

MICROSCOPES

The reason we know so much about the hidden life in a garden is because scientists have studied microbes using microscopes. The kind of microscope that you might have used at school or at home is a light microscope. A powerful one can magnify things up to 1800 times. But to get a close look at really tiny things such as **bacteria**, you need an **electron microscope**. This can magnify objects up to half a million times.

Spidery sap suckers

Hold a piece of white paper under a plant in your garden. Now give the stem a sharp tap. Some little specks will fall onto the paper. The specks may be bits of dirt and dust, but if they start to crawl around they are probably spider **mites**.

Mites are relations of spiders. They have a roundish body, a small head and eight legs. Most are only just visible. The mites that live on plants spin webs, which is why they are called spider mites.

Red mites (x330) are pests of many crops. They have no eyes – instead, the sensory hairs on their body tell them about the outside world.

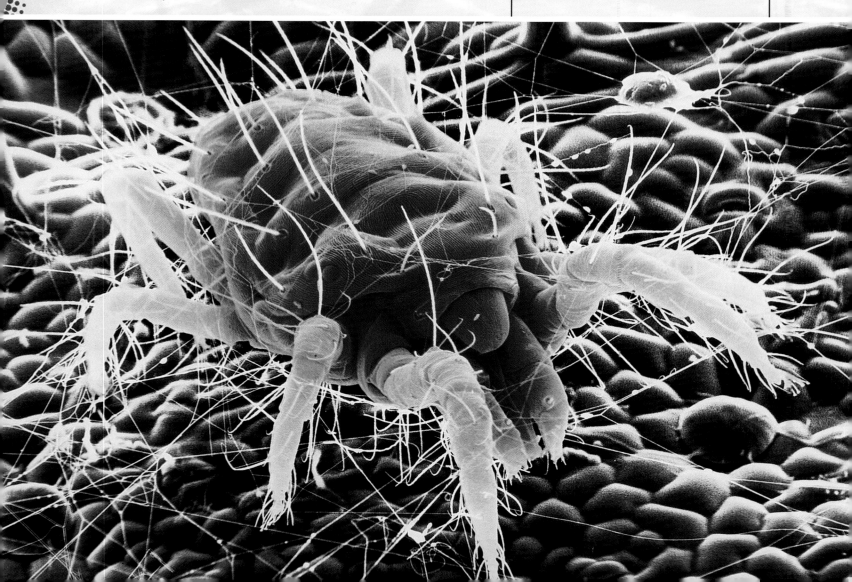

Lifestyle

Spider mites have two thin, needle-sharp structures called **stylets** which they use to make holes in leaf **cells**. They then suck up sap from the cells.

A female mite lives for 4 to 6 weeks and produces up to 150 eggs. If it is warm, the eggs can become adults in just a week, so mite numbers can explode during a hot summer.

When they first hatch, young mites are called **larvae**. They have six legs rather than eight. After a few days the larvae **moult** and become **nymphs**. Nymphs have eight legs. After two more moults and another 5 or 6 days, the nymphs become adults.

Fight mites with mites

Spider mites are plant pests because they damage many of the crops we grow. They can stunt the growth of a plant, or even kill it.

One way to control spider mites is to use other mites. Some kinds of mite are

predators on spider mites. They eat the spider mites and their eggs, keeping the numbers of these pests low.

🖙 *An orange predatory mite attacking a spider mite.*

WARM AND COOL MITES

Some mites like hot weather, and do best in places with warm summers. Females born in the autumn spend the winter in a resting state (a kind of **hibernation**). In spring the females become active and lay eggs.

Other spider mites prefer cooler conditions. They are most active in spring and autumn, and rest during the summer and winter.

Roundworms

Most gardens have plenty of earthworms. But there are also millions of much smaller worms called **roundworms**. Roundworms are a fraction of a millimetre long, and their bodies are transparent. Some are **parasites** on plants, but there are also millions of free-living roundworms in the soil.

stylet

Root-feeding roundworms often cause diseases in crops. This pea plant has knots caused by roundworms feeding on its roots.

A plant-feeding roundworm, showing its sharp stylet.

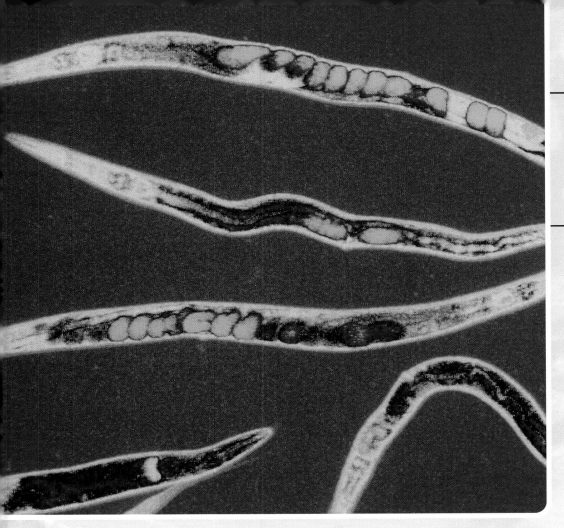

The roundworm *Caenorhabditis elegans* (x235) lives in the soil and feeds on bacteria.

Some roundworms live on the upper parts of plants, but many more live on the roots. Some kinds burrow into the root, then settle down and begin to eat. As they feed they swell and become pear-shaped or round. Often the root around them swells too, producing a thickening called a 'knot'.

A roundworm's life

A roundworm's body is a simple tube. Most of the inside of this tube is taken up with the gut. Muscles run along the length of the body, but there are no muscles running in other directions, so a roundworm can only move its body from side to side. The head of a roundworm has a few tiny sense organs and a mouth.

The skin of a roundworm is tough and flexible, but it does not grow. Young roundworms have to shed their skins (**moult**) as they grow bigger. A roundworm moults four times between hatching and becoming an adult.

Roundworms on plants

Many different kinds of roundworm live on plants. Most have a sharp spike called a **stylet**, which is part of their mouth. They use it to pierce the tough outer walls of plant **cells**, then they suck out the insides.

Soil roundworms

There is an incredible variety of roundworms living in the soil. Some feed on **bacteria**, some eat **fungi**, and some are **predators** on other roundworms. They play an important part in breaking down dead material and releasing **nutrients** that help plants to grow. They are also food for bigger animals such as insects.

Plant parasites

Many kinds of **microbes** live on plants. Some cause their host plant no harm, but others can cause diseases. **Fungi** are the commonest disease-producers.

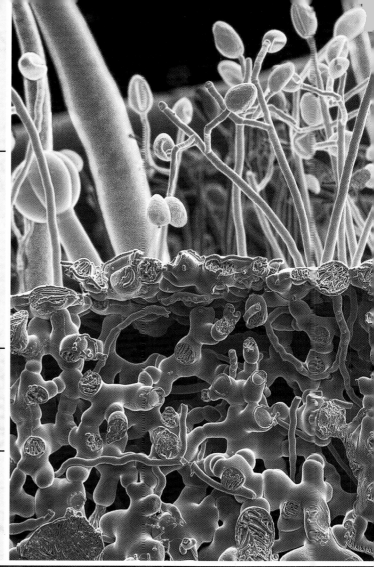

Magnified section (x252) of a potato leaf with **blight**. The stalks with oval pods on the end are the fungus's spore-producing bodies. Thread-like **hyphae** are visible inside the leaf tissue.

Leaf spot on a begonia leaf. Only the spore-producing bodies (the white spots) show at the surface.

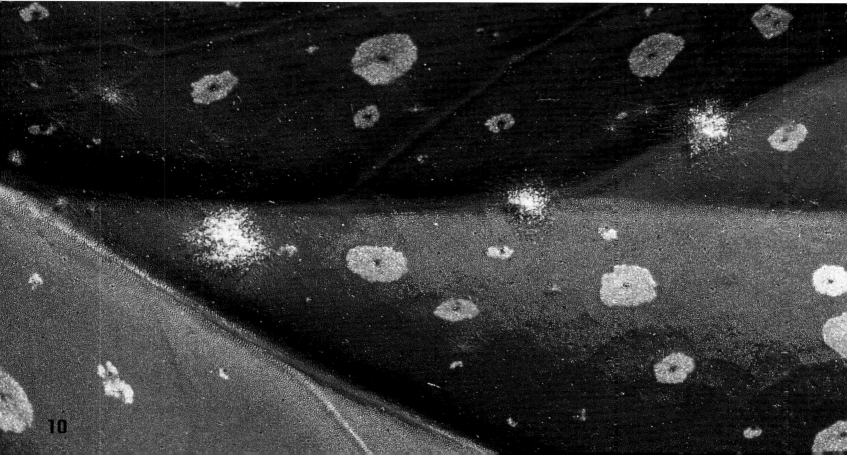

What are fungi?

Mushrooms and toadstools are the best-known kinds of fungi, but there are many others. Some grow in the soil, some live on dead plants or animals and some are **parasites**. Fungi grow in one place and do not move about. They do not make their own food like plants – instead they grow on or into their food, and absorb **nutrients** from it.

Fungi reproduce by making microscopic 'seeds' known as **spores**. Some fungi produce light, dry spores that can be spread by the slightest breeze. Others produce 'wet' spores, which trickle away into the soil or onto other parts of a plant.

Getting a foothold

When a spore lands on a plant, if conditions are right it will begin to grow. Often, the spore cannot get through the plant's thick outer cuticle (waxy layer), so a tube grows along the surface. Plants have many tiny holes in them, which allow them to 'breathe'.

WHY HIDDEN LIFE?

Mushrooms and toadstools are not microscopic – so why are fungi 'hidden life'? The part of a fungus that we normally see – a mushroom, a toadstool or a bracket fungus, for instance – is not its 'body', but the structure that produces spores. The main body of the fungus is made up of microscopic threads called hyphae. The hyphae are hidden in the soil, leaf, or whatever the fungus is growing on.

If the tube from a spore finds one of these holes, it grows down it and into the plant.

Different diseases

Different fungi cause different diseases in plants. Powdery **mildews** grow on the plant surface, and produce spores that are like fine powder. Other fungi grow in small areas inside the plant, causing diseases such as leaf spot and **canker**. Some fungi affect the roots, causing **wilt**. Others affect the whole plant, which causes blight and other diseases.

Magnified view (x280) of a cluster of spore-producing bodies bursting out through the surface of a leaf. This fungus causes a disease called rust.

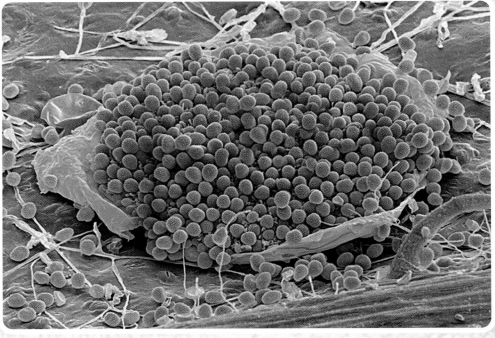

Underground partnerships

Not all **microbes** that live on plants cause disease. Some work in partnership with plants. The microbes help the plants to get **nutrients** and water from the soil. In return, the microbes get a free supply of food. This kind of helpful partnership is called **symbiosis**.

Although plants can make their own food, they need to take up water and some nutrients from the soil. These nutrients are simple chemicals that plants need to grow properly. Plants often team up with microbes to help them get water and nutrients. Most often the partnership is with **fungi**.

🔊 Mycorrhizal fungi spread out from tree roots over a wide area. Many are mushroom-type fungi.

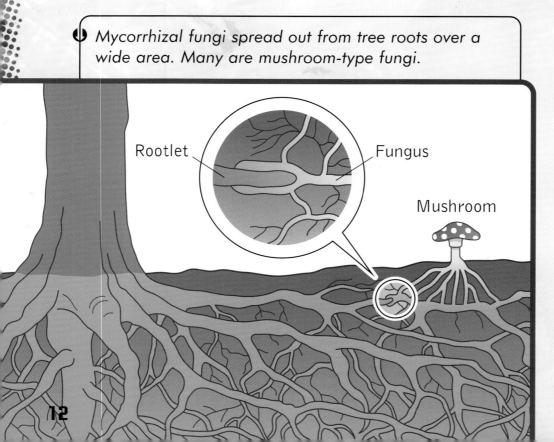

Rootlet

Fungus

Mushroom

Fungus roots

Most plants have one or more types of fungi living in or around their roots. The combination is called a **mycorrhiza** (my-cor-iza), which means 'fungus root'.

As we saw on page 11, the body of a fungus is made up of microscopic threads called **hyphae**. In a mycorrhiza, these hyphae spread out from the plant's

This cep, or 'penny bun', is the fruiting body (the **spore**-producing part) of a mycorrhizal fungus.

into ammonia, a very important ingredient for plants. In return, the bacteria get to feed on sugars produced by the plant.

With *Rhizobium* bacteria in their roots, legumes can grow in soils that other plants cannot survive in.

Rhizobium *bacteria can live independently in the soil, or they can grow in a plant's roots.*

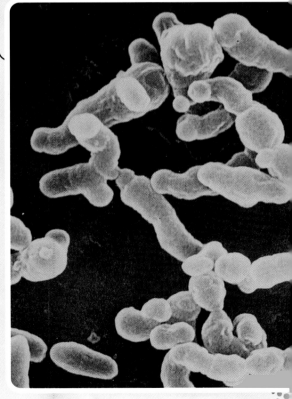

roots and greatly increase the area of soil from which the plant can absorb nutrients. In return for help in getting water and nutrients, the plant supplies the fungus with some of the sugary food that it makes.

Mycorrhizas are most important for forest trees, but they are found in most kinds of plant. Some plants cannot survive without fungi growing on their roots. Others grow more slowly if they have no fungi.

Peas and beans

Another kind of partnership is important for legumes (plants such as peas, beans and peanuts). These plants form partnerships with **bacteria** called *Rhizobium*. These bacteria can take **nitrogen** gas from the air and turn it

Microlife in the soil

Every handful of garden soil is teeming with microlife. These microscopic creatures do a very important job. They are nature's clean-up squad – they break down fallen leaves, animal wastes, dead insects and other material and turn them into rich soil.

Imagine what would happen if dead animals, animal wastes and dead plants did not **decompose**. In a very short time the world would be swamped with waste materials. The process of getting rid of nature's waste happens in the soil. Every teaspoon of soil is full of life, and nearly all of it is very tiny.

Breaking up the waste

Before **microbes** can get to work, earthworms, beetles and other soil minibeasts have to break up nature's wastes into smaller pieces. When a tree dies, for instance, a whole range of beetles and other insects tunnel into the dead wood. Birds such as woodpeckers also make holes as they excavate the wood looking for insects. The tunnels and holes made by these animals allow other insects, **roundworms** and **fungi** to get into the wood.

Earthworms and other minibeasts are important in the first stage of decomposition of natural wastes.

In a similar way, leaves, smaller plants and animal wastes are broken into pieces by earthworms and insects. This is an important step, because it helps microbes get at the wastes and speeds up decomposition. Earthworms are the most important of the large decomposers. All the soil you have ever seen has passed through the stomachs of several earthworms.

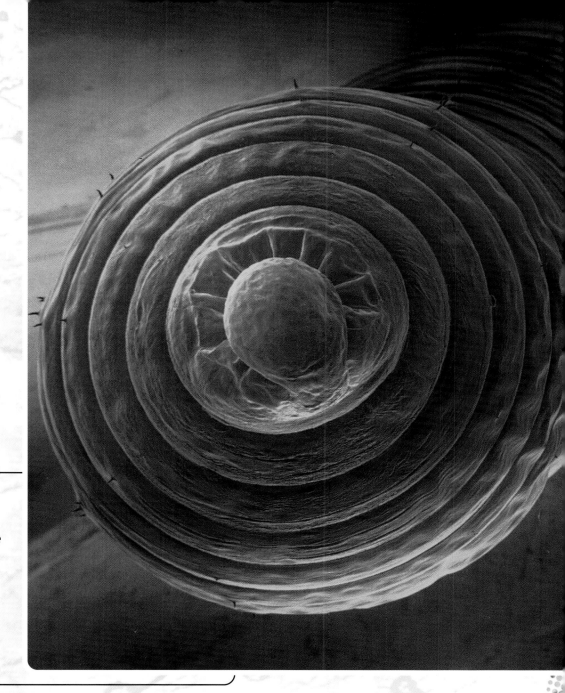

The magnified (x72) head of an earthworm. Earthworms take in huge amounts of soil and extract food from it. The waste comes out as 'worm casts', tiny piles of fine dirt.

A TEASPOON OF SOIL

A teaspoon of rich soil contains an incredible number of creatures. These include:
- one or two smaller insects such as **springtails**
- up to 5000 roundworms
- up to 100,000 **algae** (plant-like microbes)
- anything from a few thousand to 2½ million fungi
- up to 4 billion **bacteria**

A teaspoon of soil is too small to contain any earthworms, but a hectare (a square kilometre) contains up to 3 million of them.

The decomposers

Once natural waste materials have been broken up into pieces, the **decomposers** can get to work. The most important decomposers are **fungi** and **bacteria**.

Soil bacteria

Bacteria are found throughout the soil. They live in thin films of water that cling to soil particles. Different bacteria can use a wide range of substances as food. Some live on materials such as **proteins** that are made by living things. Some can use the waste products from other bacteria as food. Some can use **nitrogen** from the air to help them get energy. Others can live without any air – they do not need to 'breathe'.

The overall result of the activity of all these bacteria is that natural wastes are broken down, and **nutrients** that plants can use are released into the soil.

These Bacillus *bacteria (x2723) are common on decomposing material. Each type of decomposing bacteria can break down different types of chemicals.*

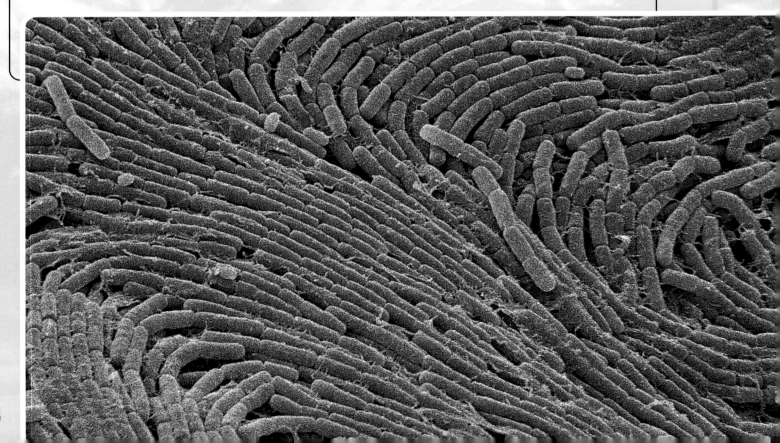

Fungi can grow deep into the material that they are living on. Often they have beautiful colours and shapes.

contain a tough material called lignin. Bacteria generally make no impression on lignin, but fungi can break it down.

Fungi are also more active than bacteria in **acid** soils. Many bacteria cannot grow in acidic conditions, but fungi can. Forest soils tend to be acidic, and they contain lots of woody material, so fungi are often the main decomposers in forests.

Breaking down natural wastes is not the only job that soil bacteria do. Many produce a sticky 'slime', which helps to bind tiny soil particles together into bigger particles. This helps keep the soil moist and airy, which is good for growing plants.

Soil fungi

Although bacteria are the most important decomposers, there are some jobs that fungi are better at. Woody plants and trees

Thread-like Actinomycetes bacteria (x1595) look similar to fungi, but the threads are even smaller.

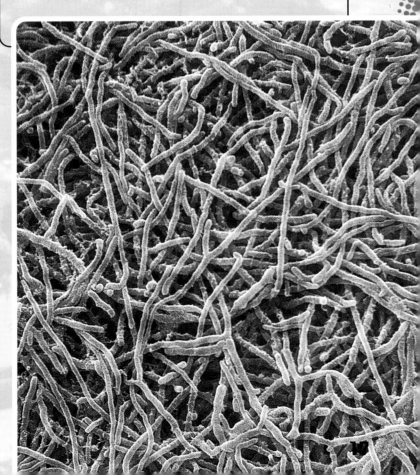

HUMONGOUS FUNGUS

Fungal **hyphae** are microscopic, but the network of hyphae from a single fungus can cover a huge area. One *Armillaria* fungus in a forest in Oregon, USA, covers an area of nearly 10 square kilometres.

Microscopic grazers

Decomposers are not the only microscopic creatures in the soil. There are also **microbes** that 'graze' on **bacteria** and **fungi**. Without these grazers, the decomposers would grow out of control.

Some **roundworms** are microscopic grazers. There are also single-celled creatures called **protozoans** and tiny minibeasts called **springtails**.

Protozoans

Like bacteria, protozoans are creatures that consist of only one **cell**. But they are bigger and more complex than bacteria. Many different kinds of protozoa live in the film of water that sticks to soil particles.

Amoebas are a group of protozoans that can send out long 'fingers' known as **pseudopods**, which they use to pull themselves along or to catch bacteria. Ciliates are covered in tiny hairs called **cilia**, which they use to swim slowly around. Flagellates have a few long, whip-like hairs called **flagella**, which make them fast swimmers.

Vortice la (x1578) is a ciliate that lives in wet soils. Its mouth is surrounded by a ring of cilia that beat to draw in food.

The different kinds of protozoa get food in different ways. Amoebas creep along through the soil and surround prey with their pseudopods before the prey notice what is happening. Ciliates do not need to move quickly because they can use their cilia to waft a current of water and small food particles towards their mouth. Flagellates are more like hunters: they can move quickly and catch larger prey.

A magnified photo of a springtail.

Foraminiferans are chalky relatives of soil amoebas that live in the ocean. Rocks such as chalk and limestone are made up of the squashed-together shells of foraminiferans that died millions of years ago.

Springtails

Springtails are close relatives of insects that live in all kinds of soil. They are about a millimetre in length, and can be a variety of colours – black, grey, white, yellow, lavender, red, green or gold. They graze on bacteria, fungi and whatever other food they find.

Springtails get their name from a forked 'tail' on the underside of their abdomen. This fork is tucked under their body like a spring. When a springtail needs to make a quick getaway, it releases the forked 'spring' and flips itself into the air.

Like roundworms and protozoa, springtails help to keep the numbers of decomposing microbes under control.

Creating compost

Have you got a **compost** heap in your garden? It could be simply a pile of grass cuttings, weeds and kitchen scraps. Or you might have a special bin that you make your compost in. Compost heaps are packed full of microlife. They can turn your waste into a rich, brown compost that will improve the soil.

It is important to let plenty of air into a compost heap, because the quickest decomposing microbes need oxygen to live. Without air the heap can become slimy and smelly.

Rich, brown, crumbly compost like this improves the garden soil and helps the plants to grow.

Many of the creatures in a compost heap are **decomposers** from the soil. They get into the compost on plants that are put into the heap. But a compost heap is more concentrated than normal soil, so things happen differently.

Hotting up

When you start a compost heap the material decomposes quite slowly because there isn't much there. But as the amount of waste grows, enormous numbers of decomposers build up, and they generate lots of heat. The compost may get so hot that it gives off steam.

Such temperatures are too high for most **microbes**. But there are some kinds of **bacteria** that love hot conditions, and these thrive when temperatures rise.

At high temperatures the chemical changes in the heap happen much faster, so the compost decomposes quickly.

Cooling down

After a few months, most of the material in the compost has been broken down and the heap begins to cool. Larger decomposers now move in, such as earthworms, woodlice, and the kinds of **fungi** that produce mushrooms or toadstools.

During this stage the compost becomes darker and more crumbly.

Keeping it cool

Compost heaps don't always get hot – sometimes the heap remains cool, perhaps because of the type of waste, or because the weather is cold. The pile of waste still turns into compost, but the process takes much longer.

One disadvantage of cool composting is that it doesn't kill weed seeds. This means that weeds that are producing seeds cannot be put into the heap, as the seeds will grow when the compost is put on the garden.

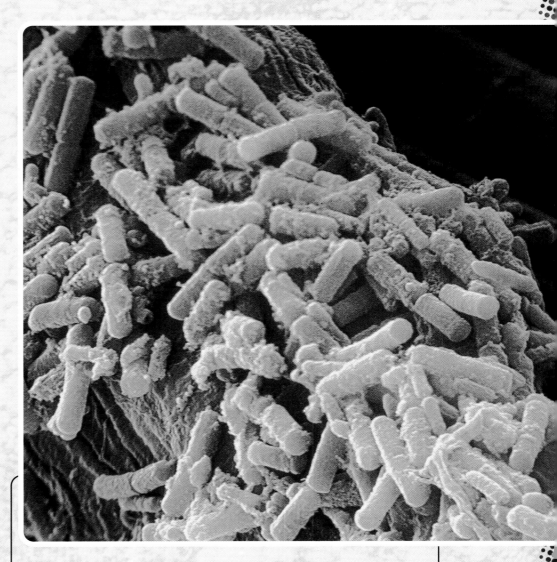

Heat-loving bacteria like Bacillus stearothermophilus *grow best at temperatures of 55–75°C.*

Water life

You may have a pond in your garden. If not, you probably have a bird bath, a rain barrel or just a muddy puddle. Often the water has a green tinge or green slime on it. These are signs of hidden life.

These 'rocks' started life as colonies of **cyanobacteria** like the kind you find in your garden. But over millions of years they have solidified to form large **fossils**.

The spiral chloroplasts of Spirogyra. They run through individual cells joined end to end to form long strings.

Some of the **microbes** in water are like plants – they can make food by **photosynthesis**. Such microbes begin to appear in water almost as soon as it collects. They may be blown through the air and land in the water, or they may come from the soil.

The tiniest 'plants'

The tiniest microbes that can photosynthesize are called cyanobacteria. They are usually blue-green, because they contain a blue-green pigment (colouring) that helps them get energy from light. However, some cyanobacteria are red or pink, because they contain other pigments that hide the blue-green colour. Red cyanobacteria might turn the water in your bird bath red!

Algae

The other plant-like microbes in water are larger creatures known as **algae**. There are many different kinds. Some join together in a long string, while others are single **cells** freely swimming in the water.

Desmids can be found in ponds, puddles, gutters – anywhere where there is fresh water.

their cells. These chloroplasts are usually oval, but in *Spirogyra* they are long spirals.

Among the most beautiful of the free-swimming algae are microscopic green jewels known as desmids. Desmids are made up of two half-cells, joined in the middle. Each half-cell is a mirror image of the other.

Algae and cyanobacteria can be a

More water life

The plant-like **microbes** in water provide food for other microlife. There are **protozoans** that look like tiny suns, minute animals with 'wheels', and relatives of crabs that are used as fish food.

The protozoans in water include amoebas, ciliates and flagellates similar to those found in soil. Relatives of amoebas called actinopods also live in water.

Ray feet

Actinopods are round, with many thin 'rays' projecting from their bodies like the rays of the sun. These rays are similar to the **pseudopods** of amoebas.

Actinopods use these spiky pseudopods to gather food. Microbes get tangled in the mass of spikes, and the actinopod then releases chemicals which break down the food.

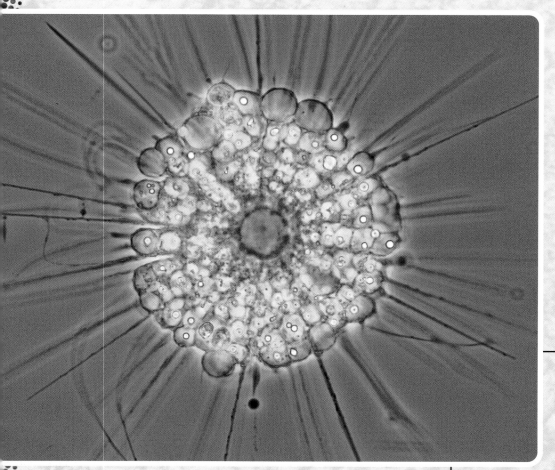

Spinning wheels

Wherever there is fresh water, you are likely to find rotifers. These tiny creatures get their name from one or more wheel-like crowns of tiny moving hairs (**cilia**) on their bodies. A 'Mexican wave' of movement runs round this wheel of cilia, making it look as if the wheel is rotating.

The group of actinopods found in freshwater are called Heliozoa, which means 'sun animals'.

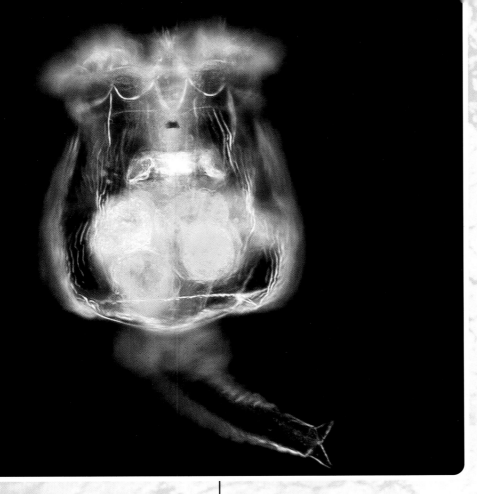

Fleas are insects, but water fleas are **crustaceans** (related to crabs). They are called fleas because of the way they seem to 'hop' through the water. They are about 2 millimetres long, and transparent.

The most common water fleas are a kind called *Daphnia*. They eat mainly bacteria and small algae. Other kinds of water flea are predators. They tear pieces out of their victim's body with their strong mandibles (jaws).

If the water a rotifer (x105) is living in dries out, the rotifer dries into a wrinkled speck. But some rotifers can survive drying out, and become active if water is available.

Daphnia are water fleas. They are an important ingredient of goldfish food sold in pet shops.

Rotifers can use their wheels to move through the water, or to waft food into their mouths. Some rotifers graze on **algae** or **bacteria**, but others are fierce **predators**. One kind of rotifer eats water fleas.

Water fleas

You can find water fleas in almost any patch of water.

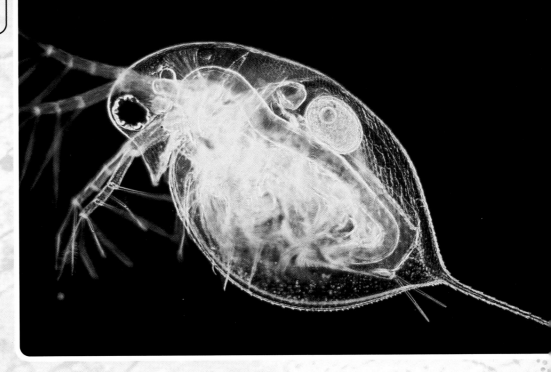

Two-in-one creatures

Are there patches of colour on the stones or trees in your garden? If so, they might be lichens. Lichens grow in all kinds of places, from burning deserts to the freezing Antarctic. Although they grow like plants, lichens are actually an amazing **symbiosis** – **fungi** and **algae** living together in partnership.

Most of a lichen is fungus, but living among the fungal threads are single-celled **photosynthesizers** – either algae or **cyanobacteria**. These **cells** can make their own food, and in return for protection and support, they share this food with the fungal part of the lichen.

Types of lichen

There are over 16,000 kinds of lichen, each one a combination of different fungi and algae. Some lichens grow as a crust on surfaces. Some look like pebbles, or have a leafy appearance, and some are branch-like.

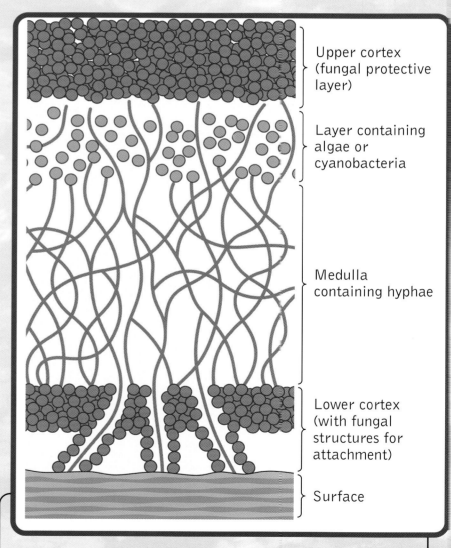

Upper cortex (fungal protective layer)

Layer containing algae or cyanobacteria

Medulla containing hyphae

Lower cortex (with fungal structures for attachment)

Surface

This diagram shows the layered structure of a lichen: the top and bottom layer are made of fungal cells (brown), while the middle layer is composed of hyphae (brown threads) and algal cells (green).

All lichens have a similar basic structure. The outer layer is made up of tightly-packed fungal cells, which protect the lichen. In the next layer, algal cells are dotted about among the fungal hyphae. Below this is a third layer of fungal cells, which attaches the lichen to the surface it is growing on.

Sensitive survivors

Lichens are able to survive in places where fungi or algae alone cannot. The algae make food for the fungus by photosynthesis, so the lichen does not need a food source. And the fungus protects the algae from drying out, which means that lichens can survive in dry environments.

Although lichens are tough, many kinds are sensitive to pollution. Only a few types of lichen grow in cities, because most are killed by pollutants in the air.

Crustose lichen is one of the few lichens that can survive in towns and cities.

BEATRIX'S IDEA

The idea that lichens were partnerships of two different living things was studied by Beatrix Potter, who is better remembered for her children's books. Beatrix was an excellent naturalist, and her drawings of fungi and lichens are still admired today. However, her work on lichens was not recognized during her lifetime.

Table of sizes

Although all hidden life is tiny, there is a huge range of sizes.
To a flea, a grain of pollen seems just as tiny as the flea seems to us!

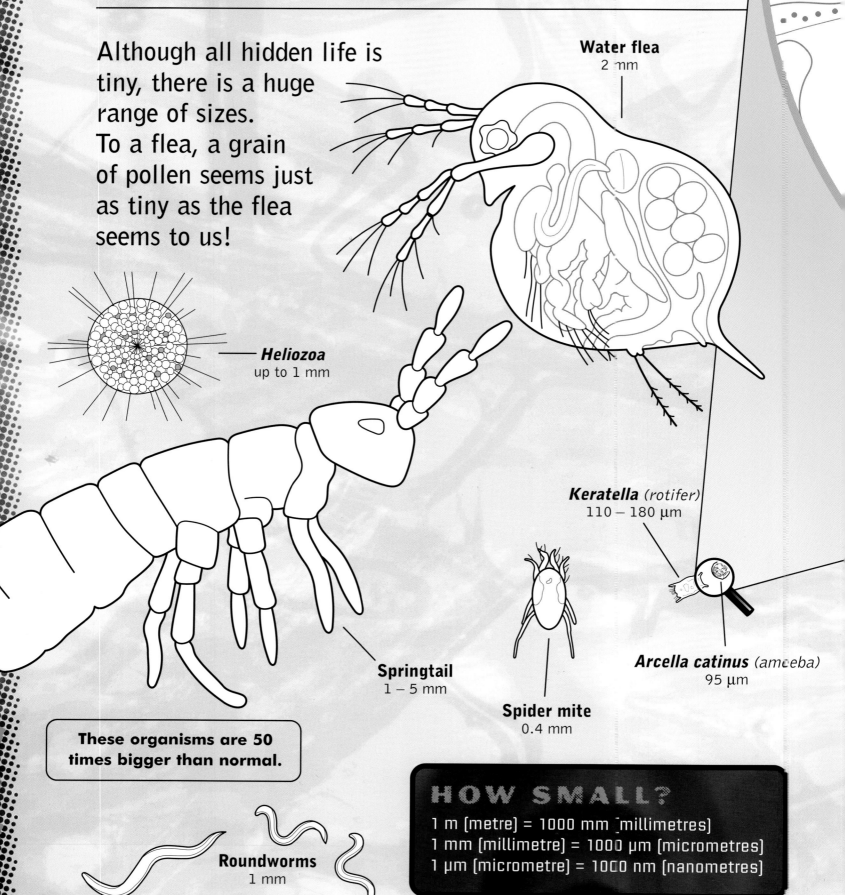

Water flea
2 mm

Heliozoa
up to 1 mm

Keratella (rotifer)
110 − 180 µm

Springtail
1 − 5 mm

Spider mite
0.4 mm

Arcella catinus (amoeba)
95 µm

These organisms are 50 times bigger than normal.

Roundworms
1 mm

HOW SMALL?
1 m (metre) = 1000 mm (millimetres)
1 mm (millimetre) = 1000 µm (micrometres)
1 µm (micrometre) = 1000 nm (nanometres)

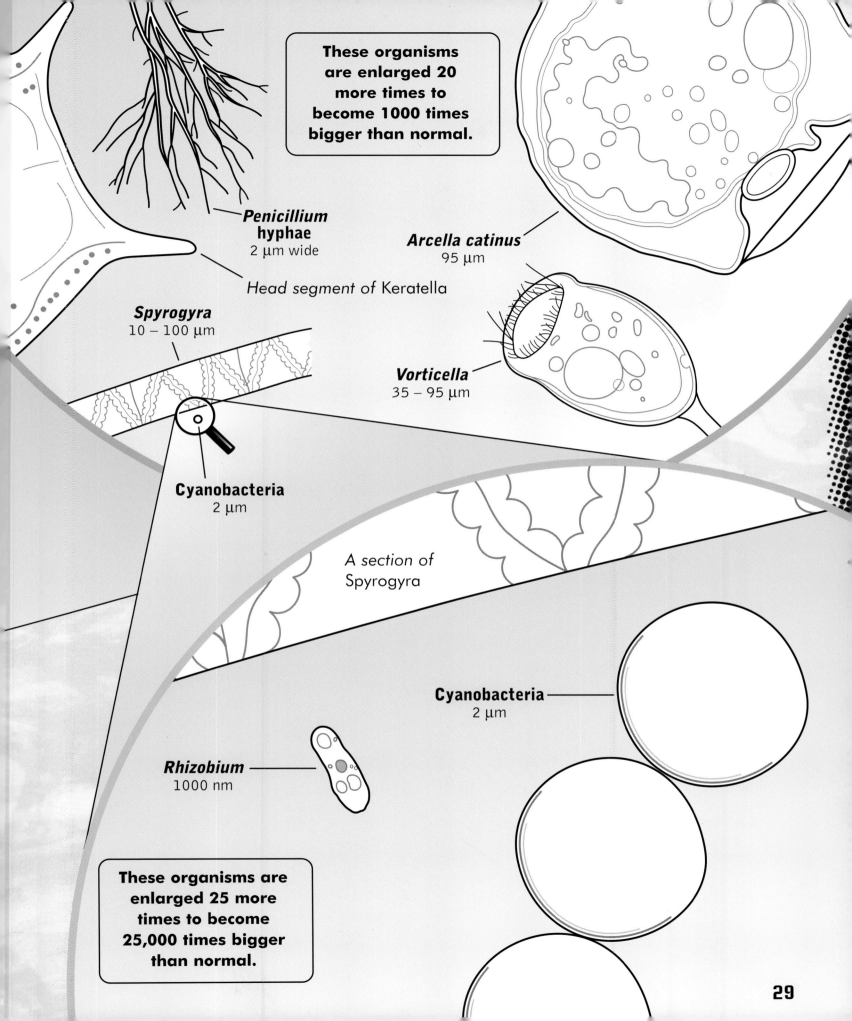

These organisms are enlarged 20 more times to become 1000 times bigger than normal.

Penicillium hyphae
2 μm wide

Head segment of Keratella

Arcella catinus
95 μm

Spyrogyra
10 – 100 μm

Vorticella
35 – 95 μm

Cyanobacteria
2 μm

A section of Spyrogyra

Cyanobacteria
2 μm

Rhizobium
1000 nm

These organisms are enlarged 25 more times to become 25,000 times bigger than normal.

Glossary

acid   sour, sharp or corrosive substance. Lemons and vinegar are acidic.

algae   (singular – alga) a large group of plant-like creatures, most of which are microscopic

bacteria   (singular – bacterium) very tiny creatures, each one only a single cell. They are different from other single-celled creatures because they do not have a nucleus.

blight   fungal disease affecting the whole plant

canker   plant disease that causes wounds, or cankers, on the roots, stem or branches

cells   building blocks of living things. Some living things are just single cells, others are made up of billions of cells working together.

chloroplasts   tiny parts within plant cells that turn light energy into food (photosynthetic)

cilia   (singular – cilium) tiny 'hairs' that stick out from the surface of some microbes. They can move in a co-ordinated way to propel the microbe along or waft food towards it.

compost   plant wastes rotted down to form a brown, crumbly material used to enrich soil

crustaceans   large group of animals that includes crabs, shrimps, lobsters and water fleas

cuticle   a tough outer covering

cyanobacteria   type of bacteria that can make their own food from light, water and carbon dioxide, like plants. They are the oldest known living things.

decompose   to break down chemically, rot away

electron microscopes   very powerful microscopes that can magnify objects up to half a million times

flagella   (singular – flagellum) a long, whip-like hair that can move from side to side

fossils   the remains or the impression of living things in rocks. Fossils are often millions of years old.

fungi   (singular – fungus) plant-like living things such as mushrooms and yeasts

hibernation   going into an inactive state to cope with unpleasant environmental conditions

hyphae   (singular – hypha) thin, thread-like cells that make up the body of most fungi

larvae   (singular – larva) young stage of some types of creatures. Larvae look different from adults, and may have to go through a changing stage in order to become adults.

leaf spot   fungal infection on plants that shows up as spots on leaves

mammals   warm-blooded, hairy or furry animals that feed their young on milk

microbes   microscopic creatures such as bacteria, algae, protozoa and viruses

mildew   type of fungus that infects plants and shows as a powdery or downy covering on affected parts of the plant

mites   tiny, round-bodied creatures with eight legs that are closely related to spiders

moult   to shed hair, feathers or skin. When an insect moults it sheds its hard outer skeleton in order to grow. Under the old skeleton is a new one, which is soft at first and so can be expanded to a bigger size.

mycorrhiza   plant roots with fungi growing around or into them, where the fungi help absorb nutrients and water from the soil and get food from the plant in return

nitrogen   colourless gas with no smell. Nitrogen is the main gas in air.

nutrients   chemicals that nourish living things

nymph   temporary immature form during development

parasites   creatures that live on or in another living creature and take their food from it, without giving any benefit in return

photosynthesis   process by which plants make sugars (food) from carbon dioxide, water, and light energy

predators   animals that hunt and kill other animals for food

proteins   substances that are used to build structures within living things and to control the thousands of chemical reactions that happen inside cells

protozoans   single-celled creatures that have larger, more complicated cells than bacteria

pseudopods   finger-like projections that amoebas use to move themselves about or to capture food

roundworms   large group of mostly small, simple worms that are found in large numbers in just about every environment on Earth

spores   fungal spores are like very tiny fungal 'seeds'. Bacterial spores are bacteria that have formed a tough outer coat to help them survive difficult conditions.

springtails small, six-legged creatures closely related to insects that are found in the soil

stylet sharp, pointed spike that is part of the mouth of many plant-eating minibeasts

symbiosis partnership between two living things in which both creatures benefit

wilt plant disease that causes the plant to droop from lack of water

Further reading

Cells and Life: The Diversity of Life, Robert Snedden, (Heinemann Library, 2002)

DK Mega Bites: Microlife: The Microscopic World of Tiny Creatures, David Burnie, (Dorling Kindersley, 2002)

Microlife: A World of Microorganisms, Robert Snedden, (Heinemann Library, 2000)

Scavengers and Decomposers: The Cleanup Crew, Pat Hughey, (Atheneum, 1984)

Websites

Cells Alive! (www.cellsalive.com)
Pictures, videos and interactive pages about cells and microbes. The How Big? page shows the sizes of creatures from mites to viruses.

Virtual Microscopy (www.micro.magnet.fsu.edu/primer/virtual/virtual.html)
On this interactive website you can pick from a selection of samples, adjust the focus, change the magnification, and use a whole range of powerful microscopes.

Microbe Zoo (www.commtechlab.msu.edu/sites/dlc-me/zoo/)
A site about the strangest of microbes.

Microbe World (www.microbeworld.org/home.htm)
Information, pictures, movies and activities exploring the world of microbes.

The Smallest Page on the Web (www.microscopy-uk.org.uk/mag/wimsmall/smal1.html)
This site includes photos and information on amoebas, ciliates and rotifers.

The Mighty Mites (www.earthlife.net/chelicerata/acari.html)
A simple and fun introduction to mites, including links to other mite sites.

Lichen Land (http://mgd.nacse.org/hyperSQL/lichenland/)
A good introduction to lichens, with a key for identifying different lichens.

Index

Titles in the *Hidden Life* series include:

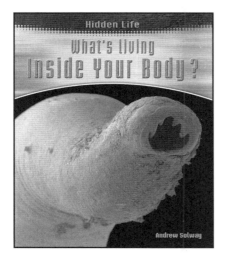

Hardback   0 431 18962 5

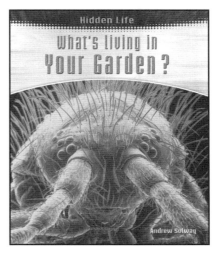

Hardback   0 431 18965 X

Hardback   0 431 18964 1

Hardback   0 431 18963 3

Hardback   0 431 18966 8

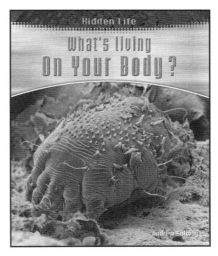

Hardback   0 431 18961 7

Find out about the other titles in this series on our website www.heinemann.co.uk/library